The Complete REBT Program

Whether you're learning Rational Emotive Behavior Therapy (REBT) to work in your own life, or helping others use it, this program benefits everyone. Comprised of nine booklets, videos, and workbooks, plus an audiocassette album, this program helps every kind of learner through print, sight, and sound.

For the learner . . .
Learn by reading: REBT booklets
- introduce you to the *ABC*'s of REBT
- help you understand your past actions and how you can turn them around

Learn by seeing and hearing: REBT videos and audiocassettes
- see yourself through others—in real-life situations
- review the videos and audios whenever and wherever you want

Learn by doing: REBT workbooks
- test yourself on the workbooks' questions
- practice and develop the skill of using REBT in your everyday life

For the clinician . . .
A cognitive approach: REBT booklets
- begin the phase of defining the problem
- meet your educational needs for both individual and group sessions

An emotive response: REBT videos and audiocassettes
- provide dramatic vignettes and graphic reminders that reinforce core REBT principles
- facilitate group communication, promoting peer-to-peer learning

A behavioral technique: REBT workbooks
- function as effective assessment and evaluation tools
- provide step-by-step guidelines for client goal-setting and goal achievement

For price and order information, or a free catalog, please call our Telephone Representatives.

HAZELDEN
1-800-328-9000 (Toll-Free U.S. and Canada)
1-651-213-4000 (Outside the U.S. and Canada)
1-651-213-4590 (24-Hour Fax)
www.hazelden.org (World Wide Web on the Internet)

15251 Pleasant Valley Road • P.O. Box 176
Center City, MN 55012-0176

The following titles compose the complete REBT learning program. Each is available in booklet, workbook, audio, and video format:

*Understanding • Anger • Perfectionism
Anxiety and Worry • Depression • Shame
Grief • Guilt • Self-Esteem*

Rational Emotive Behavior Therapy

Anger
Revised

A. Jack Hafner, Ph.D.

Hazelden
Center City, Minnesota 55012-0176

©1989, 1992, 2002 by Hazelden Foundation
All rights reserved. Published 1989
Second edition 1992
Third edition 2002
Printed in the United States of America
No portion of this publication may be reproduced in any manner without the written permission of the publisher

ISBN: 1-56838-955-8

The stories in this booklet are composites of many individuals. Any similarity to any one person is purely coincidental.

About the booklet
This booklet explains what causes anger, what the harmful consequences of anger are, and how we can control our anger by using Rational Emotive Behavior Therapy.

   Dr. Albert Ellis, who first articulated Rational-Emotive Therapy (RET) in the 1950s, changed the name in the 1990s to Rational Emotive Behavior Therapy (REBT) to more accurately reflect the role behavior plays in gauging changes in thinking. While the therapeutic approach remains the same, the pamphlets, workbooks, audios, and videos in this series have been changed to reflect the updated name.

About the author
A. Jack Hafner, Ph.D., is a clinical psychologist and Professor Emeritus of the School of Public Health, University of Minnesota. For twenty-seven years he was a consultant to inpatient, residential, and outpatient chemical dependency treatment programs including twelve years as a consultant to Hazelden.

Introduction

Why be concerned with anger? After all, don't we all get angry? Yes, anger is a human feeling that we all experience at times. The basic issue has to do with consequences—what happens when you get angry? If nothing happens when you get angry, then your anger may be of little concern because the consequences are limited. If, however, you do things to yourself that are self-defeating, or you do harm to others—if there are *hurtful* or *harmful* consequences as a result of your anger—then you may have reason to be concerned about it.

For example: You are driving on the highway behind someone going thirty-five miles per hour in a fifty-five-mile-per-hour speed zone, and you are late for an appointment. You find yourself feeling very angry and, as a result, you recklessly pass the other car. You put your own life and the lives of others in danger by your reckless driving—this is potentially a very dangerous consequence of your anger.

Another example of the harmful consequences of anger would be the following: You want to leave work early in the afternoon to play golf. You go to work early and work through the noon hour to make up for leaving early. In the middle of the afternoon your boss comes in and gives you a new job assignment that he wants finished before you

The *ABC* process described in this booklet is based on the work of Dr. Albert Ellis and his Rational Emotive Behavior Therapy.

leave. You comply but don't finish the job until late in the day when you no longer can play golf. The longer you are at work the angrier you find yourself becoming.

When you leave work you stop at a bar on the way home to relieve some of your angry feelings. You end up drinking too much, getting home very late, and getting into an argument with your wife, whom you neglected to call and inform of your late arrival home.

Or instead of stopping at a bar, you might go directly home after work in a very angry mood. You stumble over your children's toys scattered about the living room where your children have been playing while waiting for you. You *unleash* your anger at your children, telling them to clean up the room immediately. When they are slow at picking up their toys, you threaten them and finally send them to bed with an outburst of anger. You then sit down to dinner with your wife and rant and rave at her for being such an awful mother.

For some of us the hurtful or harmful consequences of anger result from openly expressing anger toward others. Extreme examples of the consequences take the form of domestic violence and child abuse. On the other hand, some of us may deny or have difficulty accepting and openly expressing any of our anger to others. We may hide our anger, keep it to ourselves—we bottle it up inside. We may be afraid that others wouldn't like us if we openly expressed our anger.

Some of us who suppress our anger, for whatever reason, may have found a release for that anger in our past drug use. When using we may have become very argumentative or behaved in a physically hostile way. Others of us may hide our angry feelings, but then misdirect our anger through outbursts at vulnerable loved ones.

Learning to understand anger and its causes
Learning to deal with anger in healthy ways, without harming ourselves or others, is an important part of everyday life. While it is important for all of us to learn to cope effectively with our anger, for some of us it is especially important. If we are recovering from drug and alcohol problems or emotional problems, we may place ourselves at risk for a recurrence of these problems if we don't learn anger control.

"You make me so angry!"
Most of us think that other people or situations make us angry. We think that what other people do or what happens

to us causes our anger. We hold others responsible for our anger—they "push our buttons." Or we think of ourselves as having a quick temper or "short fuse"—as though that's the way we are made and we can't help it. We mistakenly believe our emotional upset—our anger—is caused by external pressures. We believe we can't change these upset feelings until the "causes"—external pressures or other people—change. Blaming allows us to rationalize our anger. We excuse our anger, hold others at fault, and refuse to change our behavior.

For some of us, blaming other people or situations for our anger gives us an excuse to use alcohol or other drugs. For others, the blame justifies our anger so we won't let go of being angry.

Contrary to the common belief about anger—that others or situations make us angry—what really makes us angry is *thinking* angrily about the things that happen to us. What we *think* or *tell ourselves* about an event makes us angry, not the event itself.

When we judge or evaluate something in a negative way, we will usually be upset. If we judge or evaluate something less negatively or more positively, we will usually feel better.

Basically, we are not upset by events but by our thinking about those events. In other words, *we feel the way we think*.

An example:
A mother brings her one-year-old child with her to visit a friend. The child crawls around on the floor while the two women converse. Then the child pulls himself up to the coffee table and begins to throw the magazines from the table onto the floor.

The mother takes the child away from the coffee table, puts the magazines back on the table, and resumes her conversation with her friend. The child crawls back to the coffee table, pulls himself up, and begins throwing the

magazines onto the floor again. The mother views the situation and thinks to herself, *He shouldn't be doing this. . . . He shouldn't be such a bother. . . . He shouldn't interrupt our conversation. . . . He shouldn't be causing me this trouble. . . . He is a bad boy.* The mother yells at the child and slaps his hands, and the child begins to cry.

The friend has also viewed the situation of the child throwing the magazines on the floor and thinks to herself, *It's pretty typical of a one-year-old to be exploring and throwing things on the floor. It would have been better if I had childproofed the room before they came to visit. The child needs to be distracted.* The friend then says, "Let's see if we can find some other activities that will interest your child."

This example demonstrates how we feel the way we think. One woman was angry and one wasn't, on the basis of how they viewed the situation. What they thought or told themselves, how they *evaluated* the situation, determined how they felt.

Basically what we are saying, then, is that our *thinking* about a situation causes our anger, *not* the situation itself. The kind of thinking that causes our anger has to do with our need to control and our demand that *we absolutely must get our way!* This sequence starts with our wanting our way, which is a normal example of the self-centeredness we all have. When this wish is frustrated and we don't get what we want, we may become mildly upset.

What happens in the anger sequence, however, is that we change or switch our thinking from wanting our way to *demanding* our way—*I* must *have my way!* The more angry we become, the more we are *demanding* or *insisting* that we *should* have our way, but we are not getting it.

Self-centeredness: the need to control
"Getting my way"

Flexible	Rigid
Wanting my way and not getting it. I *want, wish,* or *prefer* something and don't get it: the consequence—*irritation* (a normal upset feeling).	*Demanding* my way and not getting it. I *should, must* have something and don't get it: the consequence—*anger* (intense upset feeling).

Consequences of our anger
The consequences of our anger may be that we try to get our way by being physically or verbally aggressive—by yelling, screaming, or hitting. What happens to our relationships with others if we use anger to get our way? How do others view us? Do others avoid and ignore us? And how does this help our own self-acceptance?

An example:
It is Saturday morning and you are planning to repair a broken wooden patio chair. You go down to your basement workroom, open the door, and find your tools have been left scattered on your workbench by your ten-year-old son. You view the situation and say to yourself, *What's wrong with that boy? He* should *know better than to leave my workbench in a mess. He* must *pay attention to what I've told him about cleaning up. He* shouldn't *have done this. My tools* must *be left in the proper order. I'll let him have it when he gets home this afternoon.*

As a result of this, you're feeling angry. You then look for your hammer and can't find it immediately. You say to yourself, *I* shouldn't *have to waste my time looking for the*

hammer, and you find yourself getting angrier. You finally find the hammer and nails and start putting nails in to reinforce the broken patio chair. In your anger, you bend one of the nails and say to yourself *This shouldn't happen*, and you get even more frustrated. In attempting to straighten the nail, you hit your thumb with the hammer, and yell, "I *can't* stand it!" And with that, you become enraged and throw the hammer, which hits and breaks one of your glass jars on the workbench. You stomp up the stairs. If you characteristically used alcohol or drugs to relieve your anger, you might go to the refrigerator.

You open the refrigerator, get a beer, and go into the family room to drink beer and watch football on TV for the rest of the afternoon. Then you become argumentative and criticize the family members the rest of the day. Or if you aren't dependent on alcohol, you might stomp up the stairs, sit down in a chair, and seethe until your ten-year-old son comes home in the afternoon. You then yell at him and tell him he's a "no-good irresponsible kid who can't be trusted to do anything." You then send him up to his room and ground him for the rest of the weekend.

In this example, the demands of the father that his son *shouldn't* have left the workbench a mess and that his son *must* do things his way resulted in the father getting angry. If the father had changed his demands to preferences, he would not have been angry.

It would be better if he cleaned up my workbench when he was through.

It would be better if he kept things in order like I do.

With these more realistic preferences, the father might then have talked with his son about the situation and shown him the advantage of orderliness and respect for other people's things.

There is another aspect of the sequence of anger. When we become angry because of our thinking, that anger may distort or color our thoughts or perceptions about the situation—just as if we were viewing things through "anger glasses." It's hard to view a situation objectively or realistically when seen through anger, and acting on these distorted perceptions is likely to make the situation even worse—or to compound the negative consequences.

Most of us can remember situations in which our anger got in the way of our clearly seeing and understanding what was going on.

Learning to control our anger

So how can we control our anger? If our angry thinking is causing our anger, then we need to work at changing or modifying our angry thinking to reduce or control our anger. We can modify our demands (*you* shouldn't *disagree with me, I* shouldn't *make mistakes, you* must *be on time*) that are the basis of our angry thinking, and we can work at letting go of our need to control. This may sound simple and straightforward, but how do we learn to change our angry thinking?

To begin with, we can take a "personal inventory." Taking a personal inventory of our anger will help us develop more awareness and understanding of where our anger comes from, what the consequences of getting angry are, and what we can do about it. A personal inventory will help us get in touch with our feelings and become aware of our need to control.

You can use an *ABC* format to help you understand the "anatomy" of anger.

A = Situation
The problem about which you are having some upset or angry feelings.

B = Thoughts
How you think or what you tell yourself (your demands) about the situation.

C = Feelings and Actions
How you feel (upset or angry) about the situation because of what you think, and how you behave or act because of how you feel: the self-defeating or hurtful consequences.

An example:
A = Situation
I come into the kitchen expecting my breakfast to be ready so I can get to work on time. I find my wife helping our daughter with her homework—so breakfast isn't ready yet.

B = Thoughts
I think she *should* have my breakfast ready, and that our daughter *should* do her own homework.

C = Feeling and Actions
I feel very angry. I yell at her. I tell her my job is more important than a child's homework. I storm out of the house. I am very irritable when I get to work.

If I had been viewing this situation objectively or realistically, I would have realized that my wife had already expressed a choice by helping our daughter with her homework. My *should's* only reflected my self-centered demands, and generated anger that I expressed at home and carried with me to work.

Keeping an "anger log"

As a part of learning to take a personal inventory in regard to your anger, it is very helpful to keep an "anger log." To begin with, write down past or recent events or situations when you felt angry. You outline the anger experience using the *ABC* format.

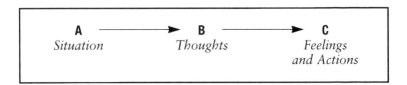

After you have some practice in writing past or recent examples of being angry, you may find it helpful to carry around a small notepad to keep a *daily* anger log. During the day or at the end of the day you can use the *ABC* format to write about examples of your anger. Keeping an anger log will help you develop more awareness of your anger, its causes, and its consequences. Keeping an anger log will also help you get in touch with your feelings.

Using the *ABC* process—turning down the "heat"

The first part of the *ABC* process of anger control may be compared to the "teakettle" analogy of anger. We can think of our anger as the water in a teakettle heating up on the stove. If the water continues to heat up, it eventually has to come out of the teakettle as steam.

It is similar with our anger—the angrier we get, the more likely our anger will come out in an open display. Some people, therefore, believe the best way to deal with anger and get relief is through an outpouring, as with a teakettle. If you turn down the heat beneath the teakettle, however, you do not have an outpouring of steam. What the *ABC* process shows us is that if we "turn down" our angry

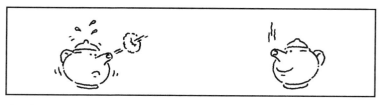

thinking that is "heating up" our anger, it will not be necessary to have an outpouring of anger. By picking up early cues of anger and sending ourselves a helpful self-message, we are not going to get so "heated up" that we have to "blow off steam."

Using *D*—disputing our thinking
The next step in learning anger control is adding *D* to the *ABC* format to bring about change. Here is where we begin to change our angry feelings by *questioning* our angry thinking—our demandingness. By practicing the *ABC* personal inventory, we learn to identify the upsetting, demanding, negative thinking that makes us feel angry. We then ask ourselves the following kinds of questions: *Who said so? Why? Where is my evidence? Is there a more* helpful *way of looking at the situation?* We then answer our questions. Let's return to the driving example cited previously and put it in the *ABC* format.

An example:
A = Situation
I'm driving behind someone going thirty-five miles per hour in a fifty-five-miles-per-hour speed zone, and I'm late for my appointment.

B = Thoughts
This person should *drive according to the speed limit. He* shouldn't *hold me up. I* must *get to my appointment on time.*

C = *Feelings*
Anger

D = *Dispute*
Who said he should drive fifty-five miles per hour? I said so. Why shouldn't he hold me up? There's no reason I always have to have my way. Why do I have to get to this appointment on time? It won't be the end of the world if I'm late; they'll understand. Stop being so demanding of my way. Maybe the person is driving as fast as he can. It would be best for me to wait and pass him when it's safe. At the D step in the *ABC* format, we start the process of sending ourselves some new self-messages to displace or take the place of our self-centered, demanding thinking. These kinds of new, *helpful* self-messages are more realistic and less upsetting and can help us reduce our anger and our need to control.

Problem solving—adding E, F, and G
Using the *ABC* format as a personal inventory helps us get a clearer picture of the factors contributing to our anger and see how to begin the change process. Understanding this leads next to the *problem-solving* steps—E, F, and G—of the *ABC* format. Through keeping a simple *ABC* anger log, we can develop more awareness of our anger and its consequences. Then we can begin modifying our angry, demanding thinking by asking ourselves helpful questions that reduce our anger. Through the practice of questioning our thinking, we will probably find ourselves less upset or angry about a situation.

When we're less upset, we can view the problem more clearly and decide what we want to happen in the situation—we can set some *realistic goals* for ourselves (E). We can ask ourselves, *What about the situation can I change and what will I have to accept?* This is an application of the

Serenity Prayer:
> *God grant me the serenity*
> *To accept the things I cannot change,*
> *The courage to change the things I can,*
> *And the wisdom to know the difference.*

Having decided what you want to happen, you can then ask yourself, *What* helpful *thing can I do to get what I want?* As a result, you begin to see what your *constructive options (F)* are to realize your goals. You then select an opinion and *put it into practice (G)*.

A = *Situation*
The problem situation about which you are having some upset or angry feelings.

B = *Thoughts*
How you think about the situation or what you tell yourself—your demandingness.

C = *Feelings and Actions*
How you feel (upset or angry) about the situation because of what you think, and how you act because of how you feel—the self-defeating or hurtful consequences.

D = *Dispute*
Questioning and challenging your upsetting or angry thinking, your demandingness. *Who said so? Why? Is there a more* helpful *way of looking at the situation?*

E = *Realistic goals*
New realistic goals for the situation. What would you like to see happen? What do you want?

F = *Constructive options*
What *helpful* thing can you do to get what you want?

G = *Put option into practice*
Select an option and put it into practice. Constructive action!

An example:
A = *Situation*
It is late in the afternoon. You are in the kitchen carefully following a complicated new recipe for a cake and measuring out ingredients. Suddenly, in a rush, your children run into the kitchen, talking loudly and wanting a snack. They reach across the counter for the cookie jar and, in doing so, they knock over a measuring cup filled with the ingredients that you had been measuring.

B = *Thoughts*
You think to yourself, *What's wrong with those children? Don't they see what I'm doing and that I* must not *be interrupted? They* shouldn't *rush in here this way. They* should *be more considerate of me. I* can't stand *these kinds of interruptions!*

C = Feelings and Actions
You are feeling very angry. You yell at your children. You call them "selfish, inconsiderate, and thoughtless." You refuse to let them have a snack. You send them to their room and tell them not to come out until you say so.

D = Dispute
You start to question your demandingness: *Who said I shouldn't be interrupted? I said so. Interruptions do happen. If I had looked at the clock I would have known the children would be coming home. Why shouldn't they rush into the kitchen for a snack? I know school is a long day for them, and they usually expect a snack when they get home. It would be helpful if they would show more consideration of my needs, but I need to also show consideration of their needs. It would be better if I didn't have any interruptions when baking, but I* can *stand it!* You now feel disappointed and frustrated but not enraged.

E = Realistic goals
In the future, I would like to be able to finish my baking

without interruptions, but I would also like to avoid arguments with my children after school.

F = Constructive options
I could plan my baking for a time when I will have the fewest interruptions. When possible, I will plan to have my work finished by the time the children arrive home. I will have some snacks prepared for them ahead of their arrival.

G = Put option into practice
The next time I bake I will do it in the morning after breakfast. At least three afternoons this week I will have snacks waiting for my children. I will also set time aside when they come home from school and show my interest in what their day's activities have been.

The *ABC*'s of anger control will probably take a lot of practice to make them work for you. That is because many of us have become "experts" in upsetting ourselves and getting angry. Anger has become a habitual way of dealing with problem situations when things don't go our way. What this means is that you will need a lot of practice in learning the *ABC*'s of anger control and "unlearning" your old anger habits.

More about the *ABC* process
You can apply this *ABC* process when you catch yourself getting angry. You begin by working at picking up the early signs of your angry feelings and using them as *stop signs*. Work at getting in touch with your anger just when you're beginning to get upset. It's easier to do something about controlling your anger and changing it into feelings of frustration and disappointment when you are just becoming upset than when you're furious or in a rage.

Controlling our feelings is like controlling a car. It is

easier to slow a car going fifteen miles per hour than fifty miles per hour. Similarly, it is easier to slow our feelings down before they really get going.

What this means is that each of us has to develop more self-awareness of the signs or indications of our anger, such as clenching our jaws and fists or getting an upset stomach. Each of us differs somewhat in how we show anger. One of the first tasks that we have in learning anger control is learning to identify these signs of our anger so that we can use them as stop signs. Then, with more realistic self-messages, we may feel frustrated and disappointed with people's behaviors, but will not get angry at them or damn them for being rotten people.

Using helpful self-messages

The next part in the *ABC* process is to use those early cues of anger as stop signs and put the "brakes" on your feelings. To do this, you can use a helpful self-message to get in the way of the usual demanding and hurtful self-messages that bring about your angry feelings.

> A self-message that you may find particularly helpful is, *Slow down, easy does it. Don't make yourself angry.*

Initially, you may find it necessary to send yourself some longer self-messages to interrupt the old negative, demanding self-messages. You've probably had so much practice in your angry thinking that it takes more self-talk at first to "let go" of or modify this thinking.

> Additional self-messages that will help to defuse the situation would be those that put you in touch with your self-centeredness and need to control. *Stop being so demanding. Why must I get my way? Why should other people do what I want?*

You will still feel some upset—since using REBT does not squelch your feelings—but you will probably feel frustrated and disappointed instead of enraged.

Initially, learning to put the brakes on your feelings may be difficult in certain situations that have greatly upset you in the past, such as problem situations with your spouse, your children, or your work.

Because of your usual intense feelings of anger in these situations, you may need to resort to a "time-out." You remove yourself from the situation temporarily to help you change the angry feelings. As part of this time-out you may want to practice deep breathing exercises to help you relax, or you may want to make use of imagery. For example, you could imagine that you have a spoonful of hot soup, and you blow on it to get it cool without spilling it. Or you might imagine that you are watching a feather floating to the ground. The use of relaxation and imagery can help you learn to reduce your upset feelings in situations associated with intense anger.

Putting it together

Having reduced or modified our angry feelings through the first part of the ABC process, we are now in a better position to look at the situation in a more realistic fashion rather than through anger glasses. We can reassess or redefine the situation: *What's really going on in this situation?* The next part in the ABC process is to ask ourselves the big question: *What helpful thing can I do about the situation?*

Here is where the Serenity Prayer can be applied concretely as a helpful guide: *What about the situation will I have to work at accepting?*—usually other people's behavior. *What about the situation can I change?*—usually my own behavior. Having decided what helpful thing you can do, you will then need to look at what constructive options you could choose to realize your Serenity Prayer goals. Finally, you choose an option and put it into practice—you take action.

Anger control—seven short steps
This *ABC* process of anger control takes time and practice to learn—as you "unlearn" your old angry behaviors. At first you may find it helpful to carry around the following short description of the process. Over time, you will learn to intuitively move from one step to another.

1. Start with your upset feelings. Identify them. Use them as stop signs. Your upset feelings are signals that you are telling yourself upsetting things. You may have to become a better observer of your feelings. This means getting in touch with your feelings.

2. Counteract your upsetting thoughts with a positive self-message. Put the brakes on your feelings. Tell yourself, *Slow down, easy does it. Don't make yourself so upset.*

3. Identify the upsetting thoughts that are making you angry about the situation. What are you demanding about? What are you trying to control? Question your upsetting thoughts. Ask yourself, *Why must I get my way? Why should others do what I want?* And then answer your questions.

4. Clarify the situation for yourself. Ask yourself, *What is really going on in the situation about which I become angry? What are the facts and what are my opinions? Is there a more helpful way of looking at the situation?*

You can then feel disappointed with the situation but not enraged at the people who are creating it.

5. Then set some more realistic goals for yourself in regard to the problem situation. Ask yourself, *What helpful thing can I do about the situation?* Be specific and concrete. Apply the Serenity Prayer: What about the situation can I change (my behavior), and what will I have to accept (others' behavior)?

6. List the constructive options you have in which to reach your goals. Ask yourself, *What constructive actions can I take to reach my goals?*

7. Choose a constructive option to reach your goal and act on it. The end result of the *ABC* process is *positive action* on your part.

An example:
The situation is my talking with my wife about our finances. We begin to disagree and then begin arguing.

1. I start picking up early signs of anger: I'm clenching my teeth.

2. I tell myself, *Slow down, easy does it. Don't make yourself so angry.*

3. Then I ask myself, *What am I thinking?* She shouldn't *question the amount of money I make.* She shouldn't *nag me about the bills. I work hard—I should be able to spend the money the way I want.* She shouldn't *always question the way I spend my money.* Having identified some of my upsetting thinking, I then start questioning it: *Why shouldn't she be concerned about the money? She is the one who pays the bills. She also works and brings in money. Why should I spend money*

just on myself? The rest of the family also wants things. Stop demanding that she do things my way. Stop trying to control her.

4. I still dislike some of my wife's ideas and tone of voice, but being more calm, I can take another look at the situation. It seems that we really do have some problems with our finances. The bills do seem to be building up. My wife does have some legitimate concerns about our finances. We both have responsibilities in this matter.

5. I then ask myself, *What helpful thing can I do about the situation? What changes can I make so that we will be better able to manage our finances in a manner agreeable to both of us?*

6. I list some options that I have:
   - Agree on a regular weekly time to talk about our finances
   - Mutually set some priorities for spending
   - Develop a new family budget with my wife
   - Review the budget regularly and modify as necessary.

7. To begin with, my wife and I agree to a regular time each week, when we are rested and not likely to be disturbed, to discuss our budget problems.

Using a personal inventory for positive results

The *ABC*'s of anger control may be seen as taking a personal inventory. At the start, this personal inventory will require a lot of time and effort on your part.

- It begins with the use of an anger log to develop more self-awareness of your anger and its causes and its consequences.
- From this anger log, you can learn to identify the upsetting feelings that form the basis of your anger.

- You can then go on to practice the *ABC* process as a way of modifying your anger by also modifying your angry thinking.
- This is followed with problem solving for those problem situations that upset you.

With the continued practice of this process, you'll most likely find that your efforts will gradually pay off. You'll be better able to control or change your anger rather than having your anger control you.

With the continued practice of the *ABC*'s of anger control, you may eventually reduce the procedure to a more simple four-step process.

1. Use the early signs of anger as stop signs.
2. Tell yourself, *Slow down, easy does it. Don't make yourself angry.*
3. Ask yourself, *What* helpful *thing can I do about the situation?*
4. Then act on your constructive options.

The *ABC* process can be a very important tool in the recovery process from emotional problems or alcohol and other drug abuse problems. The process is a valuable way of coping with the emotional upset often associated with alcohol and other drug abuse problems or emotional problems. If you haven't learned how to deal constructively with emotional upset, you may be at risk for relapse, since problem situations are an inescapable part of living.

The *ABC* process provides us with a way of seeing things

differently by not having our perceptions clouded by emotional upset. Our feelings about things change as our thinking about them changes—we feel the way we think!

Hazelden Publishing and Educational Services is a division of the Hazelden Foundation, a not-for-profit organization. Since 1949, Hazelden has been a leader in promoting the dignity and treatment of people afflicted with the disease of chemical dependency.

The mission of the foundation is to improve the quality of life for individuals, families, and communities by providing a national continuum of information, education, and recovery services that are widely accessible; to advance the field through research and training; and to improve our quality and effectiveness through continuous improvement and innovation.

Stemming from that, the mission of this division is to provide quality information and support to people wherever they may be in their personal journey—from education and early intervention, through treatment and recovery, to personal and spiritual growth.

Although our treatment programs do not necessarily use everything Hazelden publishes, our bibliotherapeutic materials support our mission and the Twelve Step philosophy upon which it is based. We encourage your comments and feedback.

The headquarters of the Hazelden Foundation are in Center City, Minnesota. Additional treatment facilities are located in Chicago, Illinois; New York, New York; Plymouth, Minnesota; St. Paul, Minnesota; and West Palm Beach, Florida. At these sites, we provide a continuum of care for men and women of all ages. Our Plymouth facility is designed specifically for youth and families.

For more information on Hazelden, please call **1-800-257-7800**. Or you may access our World Wide Web site on the Internet at **www.hazelden.org**.